W9-AFN-751

SHELTON STATE LIBRARY

CAREERS WITHOUT COLLEGE®

DISCARDED

MONEY

by Gail W. Kislevitz

Series developed by Peggy Schmidt

P Peterson's

Princeton, New Jersey

A New Century Communications Book

Other titles in
this series include:
BUILDING
CARS
COMPUTERS
EMERGENCIES
ENTERTAINMENT
FASHION
FITNESS
HEALTH CARE
KIDS
MUSIC
OFFICE
SPORTS
TRAVEL

Copyright © 1994 by Peggy Schmidt

All rights reserved. No part of this book may be reproduced, stored in a retrieval system, or transmitted, in any form or by any means—electronic, mechanical, photocopying, recording, or otherwise—except for citations of data for scholarly or reference purposes with full acknowledgment of title, edition, and publisher and written notification to Peterson's Guides prior to such use.

Library of Congress Cataloging-in-Publication Data

Kislevitz, Gail W.
    Money / by Gail W. Kislevitz.
        p.   cm. — (Careers without college)
    "A New Century Communications book."
    ISBN 1-56079-389-9 (pbk.) : $7.95
    1. Finance — Vocational guidance — United States. 2. High school graduates — Employment — United States. [1. Financial — Vocational guidance. 2. Vocational guidance.] I. Title. II. Series.
HG181. K56 1994
332'.023'73—dc20   94-19034
                                                                CIP
                                                                AC

Art direction: Linda Huber
Cover photo: Bryce Flynn Photography
Cover and interior design: Greg Wozney Design, Inc.
Composition: Book Publishing Enterprises, Inc.
Printed in the United States of America
10 9 8 7 6 5 4 3 2 1

Text Photo Credits
Color photo graphics: J. Gerard Smith Photography
Page xiv: © The Image Bank/Jay Freis
Page 14: © The Image Bank/Brett Froomer
Page 30: © Photo Edit/Michael Newman
Page 46: © The Image Bank/Gary Gladstone
Page 60: © The Image Bank/Andrea Pistolesi

ABOUT THIS SERIES

Careers without College is designed to help those who don't have a four-year degree (and don't plan on getting one any time soon) find a career that fits their interests, talents and personality. It's for you if you're about to choose your career—or if you're planning to change careers and don't want to invest a lot of time or money in more education or training, at least not right at the start.

Some of the jobs featured do require an associate degree; others require only on-the-job training that may take a year, several months or only a few weeks. In today's world, with its increasingly competitive job market, you may want to eventually consider getting a two- or maybe a four-year college degree to move up in a field.

Each title in the series features five jobs in a particular industry or career area. Some of them are "ordinary," others are glamorous. The competition to get into certain featured occupations is intense; as a balance, we have selected jobs under the same career umbrella that are easier to enter. Some of the other job opportunities within each field will be featured in future titles in this series.

Careers without College has up-to-date information that comes from extensive interviews with experts in each field. The format of each book is designed for easy reading. Plus, each book gives you something unique: an insider's look at the featured jobs through interviews with people who work in them now.

We invite your comments about the series, which will help us with future titles. Please send your correspondence to: Careers without College, c/o Peterson's Guides, Inc., P.O. Box 2123, Princeton, NJ 08543-2123.

Peggy Schmidt has written about education and careers for 20 years. She is author of Peterson's best-selling *The 90-Minute Resume*.

ACKNOWLEDGMENTS

Many thanks to the following people who helped track down information pertaining to this book. Your assistance and patience were invaluable.

Rae Lynn Ambach, Certified Public Accountant, New York, New York

Fred Ballis, Vice President, Dean Witter Reynolds, Inc., Paramus, New Jersey

Patricia J. Boerger, Public Relations Manager, American Bankers Association, Washington, D.C.

Beatrice Body, Assistant Vice President, Human Resources, First Fidelity Bankcorp, Newark, New Jersey

Jane DiFrancia, Registered Sales Assistant, Kemper Securities, Denver, Colorado

Scott Ehrenpreis, Tax Consultant, Becker & Company, P.C., New York, New York

Joelle Fridel, Human Resources Manager, Pacific Stock Exchange, San Francisco, California

Dana Gilkison, Human Resources Department, Commercial Bank, Salem, Oregon

Nathaniel Harris, President, NatWest Community Development Corp., Jersey City, New Jersey

Daniel Hay, Certified Financial Planner and Enrolled Agent, Chester Springs, Pennsylvania

Andrew Jackman, Money Broker, Traditions N.A., New York, New York

Keith Kirk, National Association of Security Dealers, San Francisco, California

Steve Lacoff, Managing Director, Human Resources, Bear, Stearns & Co. Inc.

Doug Landry, Account Executive, Wood Gundy, Inc., Toronto, Ontario

Janice Rea Marcketta, Director, Human Resources, American Stock Exchange, New York, New York

Jeffrey Marcus, President, Marcus Associates Design Firm, San Francisco, California

Stephen McAdams, District Manager, H & R Block, Overland Park, Kansas

Jane McEvoy, President, McEvoy & McEvoy, Newton, Connecticut

Mark O'Connor, Supervisor, Trading Floor Operations, Chicago Stock Exchange, Chicago, Illinois

Nicholas J. Palermo, President and CEO, Great Country Bank, Ansonia, Connecticut

Douglas Pruett, Vice President, Glen Rauch Securities, New York, New York

Adam Schneider, Vice President, Trade Floor Operations, Chicago Stock Exchange, Chicago, Illinois

Tracy Scott, Registered Sales Assistant, Wood Gundy, Inc., Toronto, Ontario

Pat Rowell, Vice President, Human Resources, Chase Manhattan Bank, New York, New York

D. Randolph Waesche, President and Certified Financial Planner, Resource Management, Metairie, Louisiana

WHAT'S IN THIS BOOK

WHY THESE MONEY CAREERS?

Dollars and cents have a major impact on us from cradle to grave. If you work in a job that involves processing financial transactions on a day-to-day basis, you will gain a new appreciation of why money makes the world go 'round.

This book focuses on five important jobs related to handling money. None require a college degree to get an entry-level job. On-the-job training is provided. The jobs are:

- ❏ Bank teller
- ❏ Securities sales assistant
- ❏ Tax preparer
- ❏ Credit checker
- ❏ Trade floor runner/clerk

The people in these positions help move and approve money, securities and lines of credit. Financial transactions—whether they involve charging department store purchases, calculating and paying taxes, getting traveler's checks at a bank or purchasing stock—involve paper, paper and more paper. Everything must be written or, increasingly, entered into a computer to make a transaction "happen." The jobs featured here also involve lots of contact with customers—some of it face to face, some of it exclusively over the phone.

Becoming a bank teller is one of the 20 leading occupational choices among those who have a high school diploma or less. That's because being personable and having good communications skills are the key prerequisites. The down side: Jobs will decrease over the next decade as banks install more automated services to cut costs.

If you've always been fascinated by Wall Street, you can get your foot in the door and get in on the action by becoming a sales assistant to a broker. Keyboarding skills are a must, although most brokerage firms will teach you how to use their computer systems. It's a good job that offers the potential for bonuses if you're willing to go above and beyond the call of duty in helping the brokers you work for.

No one likes to pay taxes, but if you are the kind of person who enjoys doing yours, becoming a tax preparer is ideal. It's especially attractive to those who want seasonal work—the busy season is January through April. An ability to put people at ease is essential; so is asking the right questions and accurately entering information into a computer, which calculates amounts owed or due.

If you are the kind of person who is good at tracking down and organizing information, check out the chapter on credit checkers. If you've ever applied for a car loan or credit card, you no doubt know that the financial institution or store extending you the loan or line of credit will check to make sure that you're a good credit risk. Pulling together a complete and accurate "profile" of an applicant is the job of credit checkers, loan processors and credit authorizers.

For those who have fast feet, quick reflexes and a fascination with the stock market, the floor of an exchange may be just the place to work. Jobs are limited; it helps enormously to be introduced to an employer by someone already working on the floor. It's a job that will make your adrenaline pump; trades are made and lost in the time it takes to traverse the "pit."

Read on to find out which money career is the best fit for you.

JILL CONSIDINE

on Finding Your Niche and Getting Ahead in the Financial World

In 1970 Jill Considine started her career in banking as a programmer at Bankers Trust Company. Two years later she went to Chase Manhattan Bank as a data processing trainer. After ten years with Chase, where she had advanced to vice president, she was offered the position of president and chief executive officer of the First Women's Bank in New

York City, a position she held for a year and a half.

In 1985 she was tapped to be superintendent of banking for the State of New York, a position she held for six years. Her next job was managing director and chief administrative officer of American Express Bank Limited.

In 1993 she became president of the New York Clearing House Association, an association of 11 leading commercial banks in the city of New York that helps banks make payments between themselves, other banks, customers and corporations.

When I finished college with a degree in biology, I thought I wanted to work in a lab and do cutting-edge research in biogenetics. I tried that for awhile but realized that something was missing. I wasn't really happy extracting nucleic acids from bunnies. I wanted to be with people.

I started to consider other careers that would fit my background in science and math. The banking industry was just entering the computer age. I had never taken a computer course, but programming basically involved applying math to business with a scientific approach.

I was able to convince interviewers at Bankers Trust Company that my skills were better suited to computers than were those of the business majors they were hoping to hire. The programming job really did suit me. I was doing what I was good at and worked with a team of young, dynamic people. All the departments of the bank needed our expertise, so even though I was only a programmer, I had access to the entire bank and took the opportunity to learn about the business of banking.

Today the financial world is an exciting place to be because it is in a state of change. Banks were among the first businesses to get involved with computers, and they are still in the forefront. We are seeing the first generation of kids coming into the business world who grew up with sophisticated computers. Everyone from secretaries to executives is expected to have at least some knowledge of how to use a computer keyboard and basic word processing.

I know from working at banks how important the teller position is. They have to enjoy working with people because they are interacting with customers all day. In most cases they are the only bank representative the customer sees, so they have to leave a good impression on the customer.

Tax preparers must also have good people skills and be able to explain complex tax laws to clients. They also need to be able to explain to clients in a calm way why they must pay the taxes they may not have realized they owed.

Credit checkers play an important research role in financial and other institutions. I worked as a credit authorizer one summer and know how important it is to concentrate on the financial details of a customer's profile.

Trade floor runners and sales assistants to brokers thrive on pressure and like the dynamic world of the financial markets. They work in a fast-paced industry where every second counts in the buying or selling of securities.

Making the adjustment from school to the business world can be a real eye-opener. You have to learn how to fit in with the culture of your company. Actually, it's a lot like high school. If you want to fit in, you wear what is acceptable and popular. It's no different in the business world.

When I joined the bank, it was my first real corporate job. I had backpacked through Europe and worked in a lab. I had no background in finance. I didn't know anything about a corporate culture. I started out by going to the employee cafeteria and meeting people who had been in the bank longer than I had. When I felt comfortable with them, I asked questions about the bank in general and then more specific questions regarding bank policy and politics. For instance, what would be appropriate to wear to an off-site meeting that has been billed as "casual"? My idea of casual is jeans and sneakers, but the bank's idea of casual may be different. You can't learn this from a company brochure.

Finding a person at the company who will help you, someone who knows the ropes, can make the whole process easier. A mentor will help show you the rocks in the path so you don't stumble, whether it's something like asking if your growing a beard would be a problem or taking time off for personal days.

When I started out, finance was typically a male

domain. Plus, most of the programmers I worked with were men. There were not many women in high positions whom I could befriend. But I didn't let any of that stand in my way. In the business world, I thought of myself as a computer programmer first and a woman second.

I looked for skills that I had that would be complementary to those of my co-workers. Many math-oriented people didn't have strong verbal or writing skills. I did! So whenever we had to make a presentation or write a proposal, I did that part for the group. They depended on me to perform those tasks, while I depended on them to do other things based on their strengths. When you are working with other people, focus on the skills and strengths you can offer that will make a difference.

The challenge for someone without a college degree is to sell yourself just like I did on my first job in banking. You will have to rely on your own strengths and skills to get your foot in the door. Once you're in, make yourself invaluable to your co-workers and peers.

There are three things you should make it your business to learn: your basic job, the corporation, and the business of that corporation. If you do, you'll go places. I took courses at night to learn more about finance. Some companies will pay for these courses if they are related to your job. I also read articles that related to my field.

Whatever career you choose, make sure you love it and are challenged by it. You'll know you made the right choice if at the end of the day you can say, "Wow, I can't believe the day's over!"

FAMOUS BEGINNINGS

Robert Simms, Founder and Chairman of Simms Capital Management, Inc., Greenwich, Connecticut

After college Simms was a tight end for the New York Giants. He went on to play for the Pittsburgh Steelers. During the off-season, he worked as a research analyst at a brokerage firm. At 23 he quit football to become a full-time broker and eventually a partner at Bear, Stearns & Co. Inc. In 1984 he formed his own company, which is one of the leading international investment management firms.

Muriel Siebert, Founder and President, Muriel Siebert & Co., member firm of the New York Stock Exchange

Siebert started her career as a trainee in the research department of an investment firm. In 1967 she became the first woman to own a seat on the New York Stock Exchange. Another first was becoming the first woman superintendent of banking for the state of New York in 1977. Although she never graduated from college, she is the recipient of numerous awards and eight honorary doctoral degrees and is a visiting professor at business schools.

Luis Gonzalez, Senior Vice President, First Fidelity Bancorporation, Newark, New Jersey

In high school Gonzalez worked part time at a pharmacy in Passaic, New Jersey. His boss referred him to a teller job at First Fidelity Bank. Gonzalez's ambition helped him leapfrog ahead even though he never went to college. He now coordinates the operations conversion process for acquired banks.

Despite the fact that banking has been revolutionized in the last 20 years by automated teller machines, banking by phone and on-line computer banking services, the majority of bank customers still have some personal contact with banks, usually through tellers. They're critical to a bank's business; if a customer feels slighted or is not helped by a teller, he or she may change banks.

Ask bank tellers who love their work why they love it, and they'll inevitably say "my customers." A smile and a friendly attitude are "musts" for this job. Tellers work in the 12,000 consumer and commercial banks that provide financial services to individuals and businesses in this country. They can be found in large head-office banks

1

and their branches and in small and medium-size community banks at the lobby teller station and, at some locations, the drive-up window.

The work of tellers not only involves taking in deposits and cashing checks but also processing payments on loans and bank credit cards, arranging to wire money, issuing traveler's checks and selling savings bonds. At the end of their shift, they must make sure that the cash they've given out and the money they've taken in corresponds to the checks and deposit slips customers have given them. One mistake can result in money ending up in the wrong account—and a very dissatisfied customer.

Basic salesmanship skills come in handy; tellers are expected to help sell their bank's services to customers. For instance, tellers explain how holiday savings clubs work and how customers can apply for a bank credit card or switch to a checking account that offers a higher interest rate on their money.

Some banks have their bank teller trainees attend classes, but most training is done on the job. You will be taught everything from the daily job functions to how to identify counterfeit money. You will even learn the procedures to follow in case of a robbery. It doesn't happen often, but if it does, you will want to know how to react. When you first begin working as a teller, you will be monitored by an experienced teller. If you prove yourself competent, however, you will soon be on your own.

An experienced and ambitious teller who consistently balances his or her cash drawer and knows how to solve customer problems without assistance can move up to become a head teller or even a branch manager. Many banks have tuition reimbursement programs that motivated employees use to take courses that will improve their skills and help them move up.

Handling financial transactions large and small is a big responsibility; if that and the prospect of customer service in a bank atmosphere appeal to you, it will probably pay for you to become a teller.

Getting into the Field

What You Need to Know

❏ Strong basic math (addition, subtraction)
❏ The basics of banking procedures and services

Necessary Skills

❏ Ability to handle large amounts of cash and count money with great accuracy
❏ Ability to reconcile (balance) figures at day's end
❏ Ability to speak good English clearly; being bilingual (Spanish and English) is a plus in many places
❏ Familiarity with computers and keyboards helpful

Do You Have What It Takes?

❏ A pleasant, friendly manner
❏ Ability to listen to and handle customer complaints without getting upset or irritated
❏ Ability to keep customer account information confidential
❏ Trustworthiness, honesty
❏ Ability to work calmly and accurately during peak hours
❏ Self-confidence to deal with all types of customers (and pay all customers the same respect)

Physical Requirements

❏ A well-groomed, professional appearance

Education

A high school diploma or equivalent

Licenses Required

None

Job Outlook

◆ **Job opportunities:** fewer than average

Jobs are expected to decrease through the year 2005 because of closings, mergers and consolidations. Use of automated teller machines is increasing, which will also reduce the need for tellers. Because there is a high turnover of tellers, however, positions open up frequently.

The Ground Floor

◆ **Entry-level job:** bank teller

On-the-Job Responsi- bilities

◆ *Beginners*

❏ Take deposits from customers and issue deposit slips
❏ Cash checks
❏ Process withdrawals from customer accounts
❏ Exchange foreign currency for dollars
❏ Issue traveler's checks
❏ Process loan and credit card payments
❏ Verify signatures on checks or other documents against signature cards in file
❏ Verify customers' account balance to make sure there is enough money for withdrawals
❏ Use computer terminals to access account records
❏ Balance cash drawer at end of shift
❏ Recommend and explain bank products and services
❏ Be alert to threatening situations and follow bank guidelines in robbery situations

Head Tellers

❏ Supervise work of other tellers
❏ Oversee functioning of automated teller machines; notify technician if repairs are needed
❏ Explain bank services and products to customers
❏ Schedule working hours of tellers
❏ Order cash from the Federal Reserve or other banks
❏ Balance money taken out of the vault against what's in the vault at the end of the day
❏ Solve problems that cannot be handled by tellers

A 40-hour workweek is typical for full-time tellers. While most tellers work Monday through Friday from as early as 8 A.M. to as late as 6 P.M., some banks extend their hours on at least one weekday and may have Saturday hours as well. Part-time work is also widely available.

◆ **When You'll Work**

After six months of full-time employment, one week of vacation is often given; you become eligible for a second week at the end of one year. Bank tellers do not work on any major religious or federal holidays when banks are closed.

◆ **Time Off**

❏ Free checking account
❏ "Teller of the month" service awards for good performance (can be monetary rewards or extra vacation days)
❏ Reimbursement for job-related courses
❏ Health insurance for full-time employees

◆ **Perks**

❏ Commercial banks
❏ Savings and loan associations
❏ Credit unions (formed by a company or organization for the use of its employees)
❏ Other financial institutions, including personal and business credit institutions

◆ **Who's Hiring**

❏ Finger cuts from handling crisp new paper currency
❏ Lower back pain from standing most of the day
❏ Risk of being a victim during a bank robbery (unlikely but possible)

◆ **On-the-Job Hazards**

Beginners and experienced tellers: No potential for travel

◆ **Places You'll Go**

Bank lobbies are usually very attractive; they are carefully designed and decorated to create a favorable customer reaction. The main headquarters or large branches of a bank are usually the most ornate. There may be as many as

◆ **Surroundings**

a dozen teller stations or as few as three or four. You will not have any one station to call your own, and you will always be working in full view of your supervisors and the public. Many tellers work behind Plexiglas as a safety precaution. Most banks have employee rooms where you can rest on your break or eat lunch. Some large banks also have employee cafeterias.

Dollars and Cents

Starting salaries: $13,000-$17,000
Head tellers: $16,000-$22,000
Part-time employees earn an average of $7 an hour. Top earners can get up to $10 an hour. This varies, based on experience and length of service with the bank.

Moving Up

Experienced tellers may advance to head teller or customer service representative. This person is responsible for resolving many customer problems, such as canceling lost checkbooks, as well as selling the bank's products, such as retirement accounts and money market accounts. Outstanding tellers who have had some college or specialized training offered by the banking industry may be promoted to a managerial position such as branch manager. Banks encourage upward mobility by paying for or providing access to education and job-related training. A number of senior-level managers began their careers as tellers.

Where the Jobs Are

The availability of jobs reflects where people work and live. The large commercial banks are located in cities and suburbs where businesses are found and many people are employed. But banks are also located in small towns and suburbs to serve the needs of their customers.

Training

You can improve your chances of getting hired in certain competitive job markets by taking courses on your own. Some community colleges offer teller courses; those associated with the American Institute of Banking offer additional courses as well.

Men and women can be found in both part-time and full-time positions.

◆ **The Male/Female Equation**

The Bad News

❏ Dealing with difficult customers
❏ Pressure of servicing many clients during peak hours
❏ Pressure of being precise in transactions
❏ Having to stand on your feet most of the day

The Good News

❏ Pleasant work surroundings
❏ On-the-job training provided
❏ Many paid holidays
❏ Possibility of having further education paid for

◆ **Making Your Decision: What to Consider**

Both of the following associations will send free career information on request.

◆ **More Information Please**

American Bankers Association
1120 Connecticut Avenue, NW
Washington, D.C. 20036
202-663-5221

National Bankers Association
122 C Street, NW, Suite 508
Washington, D.C. 2000
202-588-5432

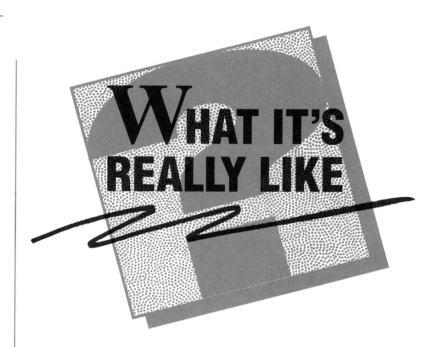

Daniel Gibson, 20,
bank teller, Republic National Bank,
New York, New York
Years in the field: two

How did you get started in banking?
When I was getting ready to graduate from high school, I
saw a job posting at school; Chase Manhattan Bank was
looking for tellers. I applied because I like working with
the public. Chase suggested I go to the four-week teller
training program that was offered by the Urban Banker's
Coalition, so I did. My program supervisor worked for
Republic National Bank and was impressed enough with
me to offer me a job at her bank.

Did the bank provide additional training?
Yes. I had to learn their computer system and know how to
use customer service skills. I was supervised for the first
day, and then I was on my own, which felt strange at first.

What did you do in your first position?
I started as a retail teller dealing with individual customers.
I cashed checks, made deposits and issued money orders,
traveler's checks and cashier's checks. I also opened up
holiday (savings) clubs for customers.

What do you do now?

I'm a reserve teller, a position I earned after being here seven months. I am now responsible for the money in the vault and give it out every morning to the other tellers. I also order money for the branch. I am also a commercial teller, which means I deal with merchant or business accounts. This is a big advancement because I deal with larger sums of money and have more responsibility. For example, I prepare payrolls for business customers. The company calls me with a list of checks, and I have the cash ready for them when they come to the bank.

What do you like most about your job?

I get to meet different people every day. When I get a difficult person, I listen patiently and explain things slowly and clearly. This usually calms them down so we can get on with what needs to be done. I feel great when I am faced with that challenge and succeed in dealing with the customer in a positive manner. I also like my co-workers, who are very supportive. It's really a team effort.

What do you like least about your job?

I used to get many elderly people at my teller station. They liked to talk to me, which I usually enjoy, but on busy days I had to find polite ways to move them on. On busy days it seems that we do nothing but take customer after customer. The lines never seem to end. I wish every customer had a nice attitude, but not everyone does.

What position do you hope to get next?

My next move would be to a head teller position. As part of the tuition refund program, I am currently taking courses in business management to help prepare me to move on. I really see myself staying here and moving up into higher management. That's one thing that's really great about working for a bank.

What advice would you give someone interested in becoming a bank teller?

Make sure you like dealing with people. Tellers see and deal with more customers every day than do those in any other job in a bank.

Kristen Clark, 25,
bank teller, Wells Fargo Bank,
San Anselmo, California
Years in the field: two

How did you break into the field?
I had been a cashier and a waitress, so I knew I was good at handling money and also dealing with the public. I wanted a more challenging job, and I also wanted to learn more about finance, so I decided to go into banking. I applied to Wells Fargo and got the job. I thought it was the best way to learn about mortgages, loans, new accounts and banking without a college degree. Also, my fiancé was going to start his own business, so I thought a banking background would be helpful to us.

What kind of training did you get for the job?
When I first started, I learned the basics of the job from a workbook. After I passed a test, I got additional one-on-one training with a supervisor. Later, I got another workbook with more advanced procedures, took the test and moved up. The more tests I pass, the more responsibility I get. And along with that comes a higher salary. The bank also pays for special courses I may need to take, such as specific ATM (automated teller machine) applications. If the cash gets stuck or the receipts don't come out, I can fix it.

What do you do on a daily basis?
I cash checks, do deposits and issue money orders and traveler's checks.

What do you like most about your job?
Working with people and working with money. It's challenging; I have to use a lot of skills, such as math and accounting. This is a very small town, so I get to know the customers real well—some of them were customers of mine at the cafe I used to work at, and they remember me. I feel I can really help them. I have one customer who isn't very good at math, so I do it for her. I seem to be able to make people feel comfortable, and I believe people will put their money where they feel comfortable, so it's actually a part of my job! Some customers will only go to my window, even if there's a line—that makes me feel good.

What don't you like about your job?

We are short-staffed at the moment. There are not enough people to cover all the shifts, so I'm constantly busy. Another problem is that sometimes senior managers don't understand how their new rules and changes affect us here at the branch. We just merged the customer line and the merchant (business) line. We service a lot of merchants who don't want to wait because they have to get back to their stores. So now we have to work faster to service these customers.

How far do you feel you can go in the bank?

I hope to make it to branch manager in about three years if I stay on the track I am on now. I am already learning how to open new accounts, which is close to the level of an officer.

What advice would you give to someone interested in becoming a bank teller?

Make sure you are comfortable dealing with large sums of money; it's a huge responsibility. You have to stay focused; you don't want your balances to be off. Also, you must like dealing with people. Becoming a teller has given me a lot of satisfaction—more than any other job I've had.

Judy Sizensky, 25,
bank teller, Great Country Bank,
Shelton, Connecticut
Years in the field: seven

How did you get started in banking?

I attended a Great Country Bank career open house and was offered the job. I had a friend who worked there, and both she and my parents said a bank was a good place to work because of the benefits and holidays. Also, banks are usually established places of business with lots of room for advancement.

What kind of training did you receive?

We had three weeks of classroom training where we watched instructional videos on topics such as customer service. We also received handouts that explained the different types of bank transactions and the products and services a bank offers, such as holiday clubs, mortgages, car loans and credit cards. Finally, we went to a real teller station and observed the tellers for about two weeks.

What was the hardest part of learning the job?

The first day on the job I was responsible for a cash drawer of $10,000! I was only 18 years old, and I was really nervous. I had to make sure everything balanced at the end of the day. I took the responsibility for that money very seriously. Also, learning all the different types of transactions was tough. I didn't even have a checking account of my own, but here I was helping people balance their checking accounts! Sometimes their math was wrong and I would correct it, and other times they would record a check in their account that wasn't cashed yet, and it would throw off their balance. Also, most of the information is kept on computers, and I had never used one before.

What are your daily responsibilities?

A customer comes to my station and could ask for a number of different transactions. The easiest would be a simple withdrawal or deposit of checks and cash. Sometimes there may be a problem with a loan payment, and I'll have to call the loan manager for further instructions. Opening a new account can be time-consuming and complex if the customer wants a variety of different products and services. At the end of the day I have to balance my cash drawer, convert all the checks to a coded format so they can be read by the high-speed machines (this is called encoding) and make sure all the transactions are entered on the computer.

What do you like best about your job?

It's very rewarding to solve a problem for a customer. I love going the extra step to please someone. It's personally rewarding for me and good business for the bank.

Is there anything you don't like about your job?

It can get stressful during the holidays, when everyone is rushed. Sometimes customers aren't in the best of moods, especially if they are short on money. No matter what their mood is, I always have to be pleasant, friendly and helpful.

What was the most unusual transaction you've had?
I've received counterfeit money a few times. We were
taught how to identify it as part of teller training. One time
an elderly person gave me a counterfeit $100 bill. I had to
have her questioned by the bank manager and take away
the money. I felt bad because she really didn't know it was
fake. And to make matters worse, I couldn't reimburse her
for it, so she was out $100!

What kind of perks do you get?
The bank is paying my tuition at the American Institute of
Banking, where I am taking accounting.

Where do you see yourself going in the future?
I've applied for a position as branch sales administrator. I
am qualified because of my teller experience, and it is a
natural progression for me. In the next three to five years
I'd like to become a branch manager.

**What is your advice to someone considering becoming a
bank teller?**
You must enjoy dealing with people and be willing to go
the extra mile to help someone. You must be patient in situations that at times can be trying. And remember that the
customer is always right.

Sales assistants are the "right hands" of stockbrokers. Soon after they arrive at their desks, the phones start ringing and never stop until the stock market closes, with clients calling for price quotes or to buy or sell securities. A brokerage house or securities firm is a great place to work—particularly if you are addicted to watching securities react to national and international events.

I n the past, sales assistants were almost always referred to as secretaries. In fact, a lot of the work they do is clerical, because buying and sell stocks and bonds (securities) requires a lot of paperwork. But today's sales assistants can be more than paper routers and filers. If you're motivated, you can learn the business (most training is on-the-job) and even earn the

15

Series 7 license that stockbrokers must have to sell securities.

Much of your early success will rest on your ability to be a good "front" person—that is, getting your brokers' clients to feel comfortable talking to you and feel that they are getting good service based on how you direct their call or answer their questions.

The more you're willing to learn about the business— in particular, the areas of the market that the broker or brokers you work for cover—the faster you will become a valued assistant. Mastering procedures at the securities firm or brokerage house you work for will also help your reputation as an ace assistant. If you work for a large firm, your job responsibilities will likely involve interacting with the back office staff as well—the clerks and wire operators who process the buy and sell orders. At smaller firms, you may also perform some of these same job responsibilities.

As a beginner, you will be assigned to one or more "rookie" stockbrokers who have not yet developed the clients and do not yet wield the earning power of more established brokers. The more you show that you're willing and able to take initiative and support their efforts to prospect new clients, the faster your own star will rise. Prove yourself competent and you can eventually hook up with a top broker who will reward you with bonuses or a percentage of earnings.

There is a lot of turnover among sales assistants. That's because the success of a relationship between a broker and his or her assistant is a question of personality and trust. If a broker feels that his or her assistant is someone who can be trusted to consistently do accurate paperwork and someone clients like to deal with, the relationship will flourish.

The most motivated sales assistants often become registered representatives, which involves studying for and passing an examination that stockbrokers themselves must take to buy and sell securities. If you earn a Series 7 license, you immediately become more valuable to the broker you work for, since you can actively participate in the selling of securities. It's also a way to exponentially increase your earning power. If the idea of a career connected with Wall Street excites you, read on!

What You Need to Know

❑ Basic mathematics (addition, subtraction)
❑ A grasp of the basics of the stock market and trading is useful

Necessary Skills

❑ Keyboarding skills very helpful
❑ Ability to follow written and verbal instructions
❑ Attention to detail
❑ Good organizational skills (to file and cross-reference clients' accounts)
❑ Ability to follow through on tasks
❑ Ability to make cold sales calls to potential clients helpful but not required (registered assistants only)
❑ Ability to use spreadsheet and graphics software programs helpful (to prepare presentations for clients)

Do You Have What It Takes?

❑ Pleasant telephone manner
❑ Discretion (privacy for clients is critical)
❑ Ability to work independently (when the boss is unavailable and clients need attention)
❑ Personality to comfortably work for a number of bosses
❑ Persistence (to track down lost checks, hard-to-find information)

Physical Requirements

❑ A well-groomed, professional appearance

Education

A high school diploma or equivalent is expected.

Getting into the Field

17

Licenses Required

To buy and sell securities, you must pass the exam (which consists of two three-hour tests) administered by the National Association of Securities Dealers, Inc., to earn a Series 7 license; most states also require that you pass the Uniform Securities Agents State Law Examination before you can become registered.

Job Outlook ◆   **Job opportunities:** very good

The number of job openings for stockbrokers is expected to grow much faster than average through the year 2005; the demand for sales assistants will parallel that growth. Job growth may slow, however, if the economy goes into a slump.

The Ground Floor ◆   **Entry-level jobs:** sales assistant, secretary

On-the-Job Responsibilities ◆   *Beginners*

❏ Help set up accounts by sending out forms to clients
❏ Send paperwork to clients for their signature
❏ Help prepare mass mailings (to prospect for clients)
❏ Answer phones; direct calls

Experienced Sales Assistants

❏ Handle account servicing (getting out checks to clients; making bank deposits for them)
❏ Register securities and prepare appropriate documentation
❏ Calculate commissions
❏ Provide clients with tax statements
❏ Help solve client problems

Registered Sales Assistants

Some or all of the above, plus:
- ❏ Give quotes over the phone to clients
- ❏ Write tickets (client orders) for processing
- ❏ Take orders from clients
- ❏ Assist broker with placing cold calls to prospect for clients
- ❏ Match up buy and sell orders

Sales assistants usually start work at least a half hour before the market opens, at 9:30 A.M. (Eastern Standard Time), and work a half hour beyond its closing, at 4 P.M., regardless of the time zone they work in. (Those in California, for example, work from 6 A.M. to 1 P.M.) Those who are highly motivated (or registered) may work longer hours to help their boss or bosses service accounts and prospect for new clients. When the market is active, everyone puts in longer hours. The end of the year is typically a busy time in the market and involves a longer workweek because more trading takes place then, and customers need records of all their transactions for tax purposes.

◆ **When You'll Work**

Whenever the stock market is closed (federal and major holidays), you will have the day off. Most firms offer one or two weeks of paid vacation after your first year.

◆ **Time Off**

- ❏ Possibility of reduced commissions for you and family members
- ❏ Health insurance for full-time employees at both large and small firms

◆ **Perks**

- ❏ Brokerage houses and securities firms
- ❏ Securities or investment divisions of banks

◆ **Who's Hiring**

On-the-Job-Hazards

❑ Back and shoulder strain (if your chair, desk height and monitor position are not adjusted properly)
❑ Stress-related symptoms (especially headaches)
❑ Carpal tunnel syndrome (a wrist fatigue injury caused by repetitive keyboard motions)
❑ Eyestrain and headaches from staring at a computer screen

Places You'll Go

Beginners and experienced sales assistants: No potential for travel

Surroundings

Brokers and their assistants often work together in one large space. Phones ring constantly, and people shout (and sometimes curse) as trades exchange hands and market conditions change.

Dollars and Cents

Starting salaries: $18,000-$22,000
Five years experience: $29,000+
If you're registered, you'll have greater earning potential since you can actively help brokers sell. It's not uncommon for brokers to reward productive sales assistants with a percentage of their earnings or give bonuses in good years.

Moving Up

The more indispensable you make yourself to the broker or brokers you work for, the more you will be rewarded. Many sales assistants become very successful in that position; their gain is financial. Some are able to boost their salary by changing firms.

Registered sales assistants have the best chance for upward mobility, both financially and in terms of their job responsibilities. Because they can directly service clients and solicit new business, they play a bigger role and are rewarded for their efforts. Some go on to become registered representatives (brokers) themselves.

The majority of brokerage and investment firms are in major U.S. cities. Small, independent firms and branches of large firms can be found in suburban areas.

◆ Where the Jobs Are

Most brokerage houses and securities firms provide their own study courses to help qualified staff prepare for the exam administered by the National Association of Securities Dealers, Inc. Those who pass earn the Series 7 license. Correspondence and business schools such as the New York Institute of Finance also offer courses that help prepare you for the exam.

◆ Training

Sales assistants are primarily female, although the earnings potential and changing definition of the job are attracting more men.

◆ The Male/Female Equation

The Bad News

❏ Lots of paperwork
❏ Pressure to respond to broker/client demands quickly
❏ Being "married" to the phone
❏ Potential strain of working for more than one boss

The Good News

❏ Excitement and bustle that come with Wall Street
❏ Brokers depend on you
❏ Good earnings potential
❏ Monday through Friday workweek

◆ Making Your Decision: What to Consider

Securities Industry Association
120 Broadway
New York, New York 10271
212-608-1500

◆ More Information Please

Ask for the research department, which can send you job and industry information.

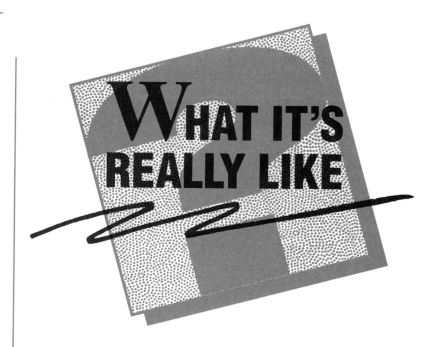

WHAT IT'S REALLY LIKE

Lori Traina, 31,
operations manager and sales assistant,
Glen Rausch Securities,
New York, New York
Years in the field: ten

How did you break into the field?
I was working at a bank as a general clerk and wanted a
career change. I decided to try a different field and went on
an interview at an investment firm. They hired me as a
cashier because of my banking background. But the job
was different from being a cashier at a bank.

Describe your job and what you did.
This was a large investment firm, and they accepted customers who could basically walk off the street and come in
to buy a security. They would purchase a stock or bond,
and I would take their checks or cash and give out receipts
to verify that we received them. One time I took in a bag of
money that was $10,000 in $20 bills. I had to count it all to
verify the amount. I also received actual stock certificates,
called securities, from clients, which I would deposit in the
vault. Usually only large firms use front-office cashiers,
because the smaller firms don't take walk-in customers.

How were you trained?

Well, my banking background helped, but it was mostly on-the-job training and following training manuals. It was overwhelming at first, but soon I began to really like the challenge. I worked at this job for two years.

What was your next job?

I moved to another large investment firm in the same cashier position but at higher pay because of my experience. I did more back-office functions, such as taking securities and checks to the vault, typing out checks and sending them to the clients, writing letters of correspondence to clients and putting all transaction information on the computer.

Did you receive new training on this job?

Yes. Again, it was all on-the-job training. Along with all the other things I was doing, they also taught me to be a wire operator. In this function, I was responsible for sending buy and sell orders, which I received from the brokers, over the computer, which is linked directly to our representative on the trading floor. I had to be very fast and precise for this particular job because the information had to reach the representative on the floor of the exchange before a specific deadline. If I entered the wrong amount or information, it would still go through but I could end up buying the wrong amount or the wrong stock!

What do you do now?

I am an operations manager and sales assistant and have been here since 1989. I am responsible for making out a list of all the stocks and bonds that the firm owns so the sales representatives know what securities to sell that day. I also check every trade that was made the day before to make sure they were done correctly. If I find an error, I have to correct it. For instance, if an amount was listed incorrectly, I have to change it. If a stock or bond was matched with the wrong buyer, I have to correct it. I am usually either working at the computer or on the phone.

What is the most challenging part of the job?

I work for six bosses and their clients! I have to handle all their problems as well as get my own work done. All day long I have to respond to their questions—where did a stock or bond go, did we receive a particular check from a client, did I get the check out to the client? At the same time I have clients calling to ask me questions—when I mailed out their checks, did they get the stock at the instructed price, can I explain their account statement to them. It is very hectic.

What do you find different at the small firm?
I don't get lost in the shuffle. At the larger firms, I was isolated to doing one specific job, along with maybe three or four others doing the same thing. Here, at a smaller firm, I am responsible for many more job functions, and sometimes I am the only one responsible for doing them. I also get lots of recognition for the work I do. Because I do so many different things, everyone comes to me to resolve problems. I like feeling as if I am the expert.

What advice would you give someone going into the field?
I'd tell them to keep an even temper because things get so crazy and hectic. You must be a hard worker because the day never slows down!

Tracy Mateer, 28,
sales assistant,
Royal Alliance Association,
Clifton, New Jersey
Years in the field: seven

How did you get started in the securities business?
I became a receptionist at Royal Alliance. It was a small company, so I could grow and move up with it.

Did your job help you learn about the market?
Yes. As a receptionist, I talked to other brokerage firms and started to learn about what they did. When I became an executive secretary, I handled correspondence that dealt with all factors of trading. Eventually, I was given the assignment of handling the administrative details of a widow's estate settlement that dealt with her investments.

What did that involve?

I had to contact all the companies where she had stocks and bonds and talk with her lawyers and all the other people involved with the execution of her will. I worked on it for a year, along with my secretarial responsibilities, and decided I wanted more investment responsibilities. The office manager started to train me to handle the securities processing functions.

Explain what you do on an average day.

Every morning something new comes across my desk. I handle all the checks received from our clients and match them with the account numbers of the stock or bond where they will be deposited. These checks range from $10,000 to $500,000. At first I was nervous about the amounts of money I was dealing with. But now it's routine.

I also process all the buys, sells and exchanges of securities as dictated by the clients' instructions by entering them into the computer or sending them through the mail to the securities company.

Do you have much contact with clients?

About 80 percent of my day is spent explaining things to clients by phone. I work for ten representatives (brokers) in my office, and I have to give them constant updates on any problems that arise, such as lost checks or late information.

What is the hardest part of your job?

Taking the client through the buy or sell process can be frustrating. They call me all the time to ask if the transaction has been completed or to find out what stage of the buy or sell is taking place. They think as soon as I get their check, the transaction is complete. But it's a long chain of events before the stock is bought. For instance, if they mail a check to me on Monday, they are calling on Wednesday to see if I received it. Then if I send it to the securities company on Thursday, they are calling me on Monday to see if it arrived. If the check gets lost or the security company needs more information, I'm back on the phone with the client.

What do you like best about your job?

I like the fact that I start something and see it through to completion; it is rewarding to know it is my work helping to get things accomplished. Also, I learn something new every day. When the firm representatives don't know something, they usually come to me, and I know the answer. That makes me feel very knowledgeable.

Where do you see yourself going?
I definitely want to stay in this industry. I would like to be licensed so I can give advice and actually sell securities.

What advice would you give someone considering being a sales assistant?
You have to be good on the phone, and you have to have lots of patience because people can get irritable when you are handling so much of their money. You need to be flexible and stay calm in stressful situations.

Kelly Quinn, 26,
sales assistant,
Prudential Securities Incorporated,
Paramus, New Jersey
Years in field: seven

How did you get into the field?
I was working part time as a bank teller and needed a full-time position. I landed a job as a receptionist at a brokerage firm. After six months I was promoted to a branch assistant job at a small branch. I received on-the-job training from the person I was replacing.

What did you do on a typical day?
This firm dealt with specialized stocks and bonds, so every day I would have to call individual companies for the price of their stock. Then I would make up a list and give it to the brokers so they would know what to tell their clients. This was a constant responsibility. Stocks prices change often, and I would have to make sure I was giving the brokers current information. I also had to enter all the information relating to the stocks and their transactions on the computer. I had to list new accounts, update current accounts with deposits and list buy and sell orders.

What was your next job?

When my company went out of business, I found a job as a sales assistant for a larger, more prestigious brokerage firm. I worked for two brokers. My most important job was to research clients' problems. Sometimes they needed me to read their statements and clarify certain items on it. Or there might be a price difference in a stock we bought from what they thought it was to the actual purchasing price. I had to explain the difference to them. Sometimes clients don't keep very good records, and they would call me to find out the date their stock was purchased and at what price.

How were you trained?

I was trained in the use of new computer software that is especially designed for traders.

How did you get to your current job?

Two years ago, when the two brokers I was working for came to Prudential, they brought me with them. That's often the way it works in this industry. In fact, some of their clients also switched firms to keep their accounts with them. I do the same basic job, but I got a salary increase and I am going to get my Series 7 license so I can sell.

What do you do on a daily basis?

As soon as I get to work, I go through the pending file—all the work done the previous day—to make sure the work was completed and done accurately. Then I generate a list of all the clients with outstanding credit balances to see how the brokers are going to manage their money that day. Sometimes the brokers purchase more stocks for them or send them checks or open a money market account. All this is done with pre-approved instructions from the client, or I call to let them know what the brokers are planning to do. In between times, I answer questions from clients. Sixty percent of my day is spent on the computer and 40 percent on the phone.

What do you like and dislike most about your job?

Actually, the answer to both is the clients. Most are wonderful because they been with us for so long and it seems as if we're old friends. But some clients start off with a bad attitude. They probably had bad experiences with brokers before and think they're all the same. Still, it's my job to prove that I can do a great job for them. I have to work twice as hard to accomplish this, but it's worth it in the long run.

What advice would you give someone thinking of becoming a sales assistant?

You must be very patient and able to handle the many client calls that come in with diplomacy. You also have to be very thorough about your work, making sure it is complete and accurate. It helps to be organized, especially when things get really busy and confusing. The big payoff is getting the Series 7 license so you can sell stocks yourself and start your own client base. Not only do you get a base salary but the potential for commissions is unlimited!

"You're entitled to a refund." It's the message tax preparers love to deliver—and clients love to hear. That's not always the case, however. While tax preparers do work on behalf of their clients, they must also know and follow the latest tax regulations. Their job is knowing what information they need from clients and preparing forms to be filed with tax agencies.

Like detectives, tax preparers are information gatherers. By asking clients the right questions and sifting through shoe boxes of receipts, bank statements and other financial documents, they figure out which deductions their clients are entitled to.

To be a good tax preparer, you have to be patient when working with clients, because many do not understand how

31

tax rules work. You must also have the confidence and authority to ask them what many consider personal questions: their marital status and income, whether they receive child support and alimony and more. If you are good at putting people at ease, you will handle this part of the job successfully.

You must also be able to record information accurately as you listen to clients' answers or transfer numbers from printed documents. Most tax preparers input information directly into computers, so keyboarding skills are a plus. Once all relevant questions have been answered, a software program does the calculations.

Still, mistakes can be made, either because of input or program errors. The ability to spot them (your client is also asked to do so) is critical.

Accuracy is a "must"; so is the ability to process a number of clients' forms as quickly as possible. Tax preparation is a "time is money" business; the more people you see in a day's time, the more money your company makes. You may be expected to prepare as many as 20 returns a day during the busy season—January through April. Working nights and weekends is often necessary.

Some tax preparers, especially those who are hired by firms or franchises that specialize in tax preparation, work only during tax season. When it's not tax season, those who are employed year-round by accounting firms or other companies are often assigned other types of bookkeeping and accounting work as well as tax returns whose due dates have been extended.

You're likely to find success and satisfaction with this type of work if you are someone who enjoys organizing and tracking your own finances and if you have done well in basic accounting courses and enjoy intensive people contact.

Helping clients figure out legitimate ways to pare down what they owe in taxes is rewarding; figuring out how to get them a big tax refund is even more satisfying.

What You Need to Know

- ❑ Math (addition, subtraction)
- ❑ Basics of how the tax system works
- ❑ Courses in accounting and business math helpful but not necessary

Necessary Skills

- ❑ Keyboarding skills (to enter information—especially numbers—into computer accurately)
- ❑ Ability to ask questions clearly and record answers accurately
- ❑ Attentiveness to detail
- ❑ Proofreading
- ❑ Discipline to learn and comprehend complex tax codes and laws
- ❑ Ability to identify important client information

Do You Have What It Takes?

- ❑ Ability to work accurately and calmly under pressure
- ❑ Ability to meet deadlines
- ❑ Easygoing personality that allows you to quickly gain people's confidence

Physical Requirements

- ❑ Well-groomed appearance
- ❑ Stamina to work long hours and weekends during tax season
- ❑ Ability to sit in one place for hours at a time

Education

A high school degree or equivalent

Licenses Required

None

◆ **Getting into the Field**

Job Outlook

◆ **Job opportunities:** very good

Jobs are expected to grow through the year 2000 as more and more people seek outside trained help in preparing their tax returns.

The Ground Floor

◆ **Entry-level job:** tax preparer

On-the-Job Responsibilities

◆ *Beginners*

❏ Review client's financial records, such as prior tax returns, earnings statement, etc.

❏ Interview client to obtain further information on taxable income, expenses, deductions

❏ Enter information into computer

❏ Complete entries on tax form where manual input, such as a signature, is required

❏ Read and understand relevance of client tax documents

❏ Explain amount owed by or refund due

❏ Answer client questions about preparation procedures and tax laws

❏ Calculate client fee owed to tax preparation firm based on preparation time

❏ Assemble and collate tax returns

❏ Furnish client with a copy of the return

❏ Occasionally verify totals on forms prepared by others in firm to detect errors of math or procedure

Experienced tax preparers

❏ Work on more complicated individual returns

❏ Work on small-business returns

❏ Correspond with taxing authorities on behalf of clients

❏ Do year-end tax planning with clients

❏ Represent clients if a tax examination/audit occurs (provided you have earned the title of "enrolled agent" by taking an Internal Revenue Service—IRS—exam)

34

Tax preparation work is seasonal for preparers who work for firms specializing in tax preparation. From January through April, you'll work 40-hour-plus weeks, including evening and weekend hours. For the rest of the year, a workweek of 40 hours or less is typical of those who work full-time for employers such as accounting firms that handle tax extensions (for people who get extra time to file their returns) or corporate work such as filing sales-tax forms.

◆ **When You'll Work**

If you are only employed during tax season, your days off will be limited. Plan on working on all the federal and religious holidays from January through April. If you are a full-time employee, you will be able to take your vacation (usually one or two weeks after one year's employment) anytime from May through December.

◆ **Time Off**

❑ Free tax return preparation (if you don't want to do your own taxes)
❑ Use of your firm's tax software to prepare your own taxes
❑ Free electronic filing (so you'll get your refund check back faster)
❑ Health care benefits (for full-time employees of accounting firms)

◆ **Perks**

❑ Tax preparation firms and franchises
❑ Accounting firms

◆ **Who's Hiring**

❑ Back and shoulder strain (if your chair, desk height and monitor position are not adjusted properly)
❑ Stress-related symptoms (especially headaches)
❑ Eyestrain and headaches from staring at a computer screen

◆ **On-the-Job-Hazards**

Places You'll Go

Beginners and experienced tax preparers: No potential beyond local travel

Some experienced tax preparers visit the offices of clients to gather tax information or go to the offices of taxing authorities when their clients are undergoing an audit.

Surroundings

Tax preparers work in offices that range from nicely decorated interiors to storefront surroundings. You may work in a small, simply furnished office when interviewing clients. Or you may share your space with dozens of other preparers, with only partitions for privacy.

Dollars and Cents

Starting salaries: $17,000-$20,000
Five years experience: $20,000-$24,000
Top earners: $25,000-$30,000

Salary levels are generally higher at larger accounting firms and banks. Tax preparation firms often pay their part-time employees on an hourly basis. A beginner receives anywhere from $7 to $9 an hour. An experienced tax preparer can earn $10 to $15 an hour, and a top earner can earn $20 an hour during tax season. Some pay a starting salary just above minimum wage, with commissions based on the number of returns completed in a day.

Moving Up

Tax preparers can move up in several ways. Those who are experienced and have proved their competence and talent for working well with clients may take on more complex individual returns or work with small businesses. Another path, for those who are particularly good at training, scheduling and problem solving, is becoming an office supervisor. A third possibility is becoming a quality-control supervisor, who does the final review of the tax forms. Becoming an enrolled agent by taking the special enrollment exam sponsored by the Internal Revenue Service is another way to gain status and responsibility. Some experienced tax preparers eventually open up their own offices.

Tax preparation offices mirror population centers; the more people there are, the higher the concentration of such firms. Accounting firms are often located near businesses, which are their main clients. Commercial banks with trust and estate-planning divisions are also located in the major cities.

◆ **Where the Jobs Are**

Most training is on-the-job. However, high school and business school courses in accounting and bookkeeping skills can be useful, both in getting hired and in learning what's needed to do the job.

Some of the large tax-preparation chains offer courses for a fee at their regional offices. Check your telephone directory for an office near you.

◆ **Training**

Tax preparers are predominantly women, especially those who work in part-time positions. Both men and women can be found in full-time positions in accounting firms.

◆ **The Male/Female Equation**

The Bad News

❑ Long hours during tax time
❑ Clients can be difficult
❑ Busy seasons are very stressful
❑ Work is repetitive

The Good News

❑ Part-time job opportunities available
❑ Potential for earning commissions
❑ Minimal training required
❑ Saving clients money brings job satisfaction

◆ **Making Your Decision: What to Consider**

The National Association of Tax Practitioners
720 Association Drive
Appleton, WI 54914
414-749-1040

Write for free information on tax-preparation job functions and responsibilities.

◆ **More Information Please**

Roberta Riveros, 23,
tax preparer, Robert Rubenstein Firm,
Fair Lawn, New Jersey
Years in the field: two

What kind of preparation did you have for working as a tax preparer?
I enjoyed and did well with accounting courses in high school and college and at a business school. I did some career testing, and accounting kept coming up as my ideal job.

What was your first job?
I worked in the accounts receivable department of a book publisher. The job was not challenging, and the pay was low. I found my current job through a listing at the job placement office of a business school I had attended.

What exactly do you do?
When clients come in, I go over all their tax information for the year and review their previous year's tax return. They give me all their paperwork, such as their W-2 forms (which reflect earned income), as well as other tax income schedules from stocks or other reported income, receipts, mortgage interest statements, property tax statements,

number of dependents, whether they own or rent their home and any other proof of claims they are putting down on the forms.

Then I enter all the information on the computer, which does the calculations. Sometimes it takes 30 minutes; other times it may take up to two hours, depending on the number of schedule forms that need to be filed.

Once the calculations are complete, the clients have to proofread the return for accuracy. I explain the amount they will owe or the refund they will receive. Then the computer returns are sent by disk to our quality-control office for further checking. When that's done, two or three days later, I receive a printout of the return, and the client comes back in and signs it. It's their responsibility to mail it to the Internal Revenue Service or state agency.

What is the most difficult part of the job?

The job isn't too difficult, but the clients can be! Some think I work for the Internal Revenue Service and think I am going to question them, or worse, audit them! I tell them they are ultimately responsible for their own taxes— I'm just there to help them do the best job possible. For instance, if their salary didn't change but they got a bonus, they don't realize that they are taxed on the bonus as well as their salary. I show them the tax tables and explain withholding tax procedures.

What is the most challenging aspect of the job?

Most people don't know what's permissible and what's not. It's a challenge to explain how taxes work and how I can help them save money by going over their paperwork. One client didn't understand what his deductions were and hadn't listed anything. After we went through all his papers, I located a number of them, and instead of owing the government money, he got a refund.

Is working as a tax preparer your only job?

No. In addition to working here part time, I also work part time at a CPA (certified public accounting) firm and at another specialized tax firm. During tax season, I pretty much do the same thing at all three places. Of course, each firm trains me to do the job their way. But in each job, I use computer software programs, which makes the work much easier for me.

What do you do when it's not tax season?
I do company payrolls as well as other accounting and bookkeeping functions.

What advice would you have for someone thinking about getting into the tax field?
If you take an accounting course in high school or business school and you like it and are good at it, you'll like this type of work. The field is very consistent, meaning that what you study and learn is exactly like the job you'll be doing. If you are good with figures and are organized and accurate, you'll make a good tax preparer.

Jeffrey Kukowski, 24, tax preparer, H & R Block, Shawnee, Kansas
Years in the field: four

How did you get into the field?
When I was 21 years old, I purchased my first house. I knew that owning a house would make my tax returns more complicated, so I decided to learn how to do tax preparation on my own, instead of paying someone to do it for me.

I took a 12-week course offered by H & R Block. Anyone who scores 80 percent or higher on the final exam at the end of the course is a candidate the company is willing to consider for a job. I did well and was hired to become a tax preparer. Every year they offer a refresher course, which I take to keep current with the new tax rules. It also teaches us how to prepare the more difficult returns, such as a business return as opposed to a personal or a partnership return.

Did anything in your background prepare you for working with numbers and formulas?
I took two years of high school accounting and did real well in it.

Do you work full time at your job?
I work the 4 P.M. to 9 P.M. shift here from January 1 through

April 15. I also work at a financial services company as a financial planner and at an electronics firm building ground-based air navigational aids. I also have my own disc jockey company.

What do you do as a tax preparer?

When I started, I was assigned the walk-ins, people with no appointments whose forms are relatively simple to prepare. Some take only 15 minutes. I ask them all the questions I need to fill out their form, then enter this information into a computer. Next, I break out any deductions and put things in the proper columns; the computer figures out the rest. The software program totals the numbers and tells me either what the client owes or the refund amount due.

What's the next step?

I review the form with the client to make sure it is correct. I double-check the taxable items and the deductions for accuracy. Then I tell them either what they owe or the amount of the refund. After everything has been agreed to, the client signs the form.

Sometimes they ask me to review certain paperwork for them that they've received from the Internal Revenue Service or perhaps from their state or local government office. Sometimes I go over the entire tax form with them and explain all the details. Some people come in and think they are going to pay the same amount they did the previous year, but they don't realize that the tax laws change. And sometimes they change jobs and use a different withholding tax status.

What is the hardest aspect of your job?

Two things: First, there are people who try to deceive me. I know they are not telling me the truth, but there is not much I can do about it. I'm not there to audit them or question their numbers, but when they tell me they only make $2,000 a year and support three kids, it seems suspicious.

The second thing is seeing how naive people are about their taxes. Most people don't have a clue about how to manage their money. They don't even know what kinds of deductions they are eligible for.

What do you like about your job?

41

It's really rewarding when I can save people money! Most people come in thinking they are going to have to pay the government a big sum. But after I review their financial history and uncover deductions they didn't know about, I end up getting them a refund. Also, each time I prepare a tax return, I am learning more, which helps me!

What kind of person is likely to be a good tax preparer?
Someone who likes to organize and manage money. You also have to show your clients that you care and want to save them a few tax dollars.

What advice would you give someone considering the field?
Start learning the business by doing your own tax returns. I have a much better understanding of how I spend money and how to save and manage my own money because I do mine.

Stephanie Fresilli, 30,
tax preparer, Tax Express,
Bridgeport, Connecticut
Years in the field: ten

How did you get started in your career?
I started working right after high school, so of course I had to start paying taxes. I taught myself how to prepare the forms. I had taken a few accounting courses in high school, so it wasn't that difficult. Pretty soon I was doing tax preparation for my family and friends. I also took an H & R Block seminar in tax preparation.

How did you get your current job?
During high school I did all kinds of accounting work as an intern at a local manufacturing firm. They hired me full time when I graduated, but I got laid off because of the economy. Because of my background, I got hired by Tax Express.

Did you get any on-the-job training?
Tax Express taught me how to use their software and taught me how they organize the office and workload. We are also taught how to deal with clients.

Describe what you do on the job.
We take both walk-in business and appointments. Right now I am averaging 20 returns a day. The average time to complete a return can vary from 10 minutes for a simple one to 45 minutes for a more complex one. Everything is done on the computer. Clients sit down at my desk, and we go over questions needed to prepare the form.

Then we review all the paperwork they've brought with them. I need some of the basic forms, such as the W-2 wage-earning statement they receive from their employer. Then I enter everything on the computer, which automatically formats it. The second part of the preparation is reviewing the data as it comes off the computer. The client and I both review it for accuracy. Sometimes they ask many questions regarding the form and the amount. I go over all the numbers with them and explain why they owe the amount, if that's the case. Sometimes they are entitled to a refund, and that makes them happy!

What's the hardest part of your job?
The hardest part is also the best part, and that's the people. A big part of this job is being patient and explaining every detail of the tax system and how it works. Most people don't understand the deductions they are entitled to. Sometimes they get angry with me and want to know why they have to pay the amount. I try to calm them and go over everything again.

I've learned how to build up clients' confidence and trust in me, which is important because I ask them very personal questions. It's rewarding to work with nice people who realize I am trying to help them, especially if I am able to get them a refund by researching their deduction eligibility.

The final part of the preparation is figuring out the return part. If the client has to pay the government, my job is done. We both sign the form, I calculate what they owe Tax Express for the services and they pay us and leave. If the client is expecting a refund, they can do the normal mailing to the IRS and wait six to eight weeks for the refund check, or, for a fee, they can have it done electronically and get their refund either in 48 hours or in three to four weeks. If they choose to do it electronically, I set it up for them.

What advice would you give someone thinking about becoming a tax preparer?
You must be very conscientious and care about people. Having good face-to-face communications skills is very important. Patience is also important, because you really have to explain things over and over again to most people. You have to be good with numbers and also be willing to keep up with tax laws and changes by taking refresher courses.

This is a great job because it allows for part-time scheduling, and the skills are transferable to other jobs.

Credit checkers are the Sherlock Holmeses of the lending world. Equipped with a telephone, a computer and permission from loan and credit card applicants, they talk to employers, credit reporting agencies and banks to find out who is or is not a good credit risk. If you like tracking down information and have a pleasant phone personality, chances are you'll make a good credit checker.

N eed money to buy a car, a house or an expensive entertainment system? Many stores, banks and credit card companies will give you a loan or extend a line of credit provided you have a track record of paying your bills on time. It is the job of credit checkers (also called credit clerks or loan

47

processors) to assemble the paperwork and verify information you provide on your application.

Credit checkers may interview applicants in person or over the phone or get a file containing that information from someone who works directly with clients.

Most of their time is spent in front of the computer and on the phone verifying that information with the employers, banks, stores and credit card companies that applicants have listed. They also confirm information with credit reporting bureaus, which provide records about applicants' outstanding loans and late payments, how many forms of credit they have and many other details of their financial past.

Once credit checkers and loan processors have tracked down all the needed information and confirmed that it is accurate, they give the completed file to an underwriter or loan or credit manager for approval.

Most credit checkers and loan processors work for banks, mortgage companies and car manufacturers that now finance cars through their dealerships and offer credit cards. Some credit checkers, however, work for retail or wholesale companies. A related retail job is that of credit authorizer, a person who has the authority to approve a store credit card (which involves a relatively modest line of credit) or authorize a purchase.

Credit checkers might also work for credit reporting bureaus and compile credit data and reports that are requested by their clients—financial and retail institutions.

Most training is on-the-job, although it doesn't hurt to know something about the business you work for, whether it's retail sales or home or car financing.

Loan and credit clerks have the greatest earning potential; mortgage loan processing clerks can even earn bonuses for each loan they've worked on that's approved. Credit checkers earn less than loan and credit clerks but more than credit authorizers.

If being a financial detective sounds intriguing, read on!

What You Need to Know

- ❏ Basic math
- ❏ Familiarity with tax returns (loan processors)
- ❏ Basic understanding of real estate transactions (mortgage loan processing clerks)
- ❏ Familiarity with credit card and loan terminology helpful

Necessary Skills

- ❏ Good listening skills
- ❏ An eye for detail (to accurately compare data on credit bureau reports with information on applications)
- ❏ Accuracy and thoroughness
- ❏ Good phone manner
- ❏ Ability to ask questions clearly

Do You Have What It Takes?

- ❏ Ability to work independently
- ❏ Persistence
- ❏ Ability to stay calm and helpful when customers get irritated or angry
- ❏ Ability to think logically when making quick-response credit decisions (credit authorizers only)

Physical Requirements

- ❏ Pleasant and authoritative phone voice
- ❏ Endurance to sit for hours at a stretch

Education

A high school diploma or equivalent is usually required.

Licenses Required

None

◆ Getting into the Field

**Job
Outlook**

◆ **Job opportunities:** variable, depending on the position

The outlook is rosy for credit and loan clerks who work for financial institutions because their work requires personal contact that computers cannot replace and the number of financial institutions granting credit and loans is expected to grow. The demand for loan and credit clerks is highest when interest rates are declining or low, since more people take out loans and mortgages then.

Jobs for credit checkers are expected to grow more slowly than average, although openings are expected to be more plentiful in financial institutions, where greater customer contact is required. Prospects aren't as bright in the retail trade and credit bureaus because job functions are becoming more computerized.

Even though retail stores will increase in number, there will be fewer jobs for credit authorizers because of the increased use of computers.

**The Ground
Floor**

◆ **Entry-level jobs:** credit checker, credit authorizer, credit and loan clerk

**On-the-Job
Responsi-
bilities**

◆ *Credit Checkers and Clerks*

❏ Contact applicants if information is missing
❏ Verify application information with employers, banks, credit card companies
❏ Compare credit bureau report with information supplied by applicant

Credit Authorizers (retail stores)

❏ Authorize a new account or extend a line of credit
❏ Give approval for (or deny) new charges on request
❏ Answer salespeople's credit-related questions about a customer
❏ Cancel credit card at request of applicant

Mortgage Loan Processing Clerk

In addition to the responsibilities of credit checkers and clerks:
- ❏ Order appraisals of property to be purchased
- ❏ Order and follow through on property title search
- ❏ Update applicants on status of mortgage application

Experienced Credit Checkers

All of the above, plus:
- ❏ Train new staff
- ❏ Assist other staff members with problems
- ❏ Evaluate applicants requesting a higher level of credit (credit authorizers)
- ❏ Process mortgage applications of important customers or those with complex files

Credit checkers generally work a nine-to-five schedule. Being a loan processor for a bank or financial institution may involve working evening or weekend hours when applications increase just before an anticipated rise in interest rates. Spring and summer are particularly busy for loan processors handling home mortgage applications.

Credit checkers and authorizers who work for retail stores (many of whom work part time) must be available when the stores are open. The Christmas shopping season and store sale days are the likeliest overtime periods for retail credit authorizers, who may work any time the store is open, including nights and weekends. Banks and other financial service companies that offer 24-hour phone service are most likely to rotate their authorizers on round-the-clock shifts.

◆ **When You'll Work**

After one year of full-time employment, many employers will give you one or two weeks of paid vacation, plus the major holidays.

◆ **Time Off**

Perks

❏ Discount on store goods (retail credit authorizers)
❏ Free checking accounts and discounts on fees related to bank credit cards (those who work for banks)
❏ Discounts on fees associated with obtaining a mortgage process (mortgage loan processors)
❏ Health insurance (full-time employees only)

Who's Hiring

❏ Commercial banks
❏ Savings and loan associations
❏ Credit unions
❏ Other financial institutions, such as mortgage lenders
❏ Mortgage brokers (hire mortgage loan processors)
❏ Retail stores and wholesale firms
❏ Automobile manufacturers

On-the-Job-Hazards

❏ Back and shoulder strain (if your chair, desk height and monitor position are not adjusted properly)
❏ Stress-related symptoms (credit and loan clerks whose jobs may be stressful because of deadlines that need to be met)

Places You'll Go

Beginners and experienced credit checkers: no potential for travel

Surroundings

Most credit checkers, loan processors and credit authorizers work in "back room" offices. There's a good chance that you will work in a cubicle in a large space shared with your co-workers and that there will be no windows. Although much of your time will be spent on the phone, you'll probably wear a headset, which beeps you when a calling is coming in.

Dollars and Cents

Starting salaries for credit checkers: $14,000-$18,200
Two to three years experience: $20,000-$24,000
Starting salaries for loan and credit clerks: $13,000-$15,000
Two or more years experience: $20,000-$28,000+
Salaries for credit authorizers: $13,000-$16,000

If you prove your competence, you can move into a position as a senior credit checker or loan processor. By proving your skill at helping to train and work with others, you may eventually be tapped to become a supervisor of a credit or loan department. To move into a higher management position, more education—in particular, a college degree with a concentration in credit management—is often advisable.

◆ **Moving Up**

Banks and financial service companies are concentrated in major metropolitan areas but can be found anywhere where there are concentrations of customers. Those who work for retail, wholesale or automotive companies are not necessarily located near or at the corporation headquarters and may in fact work in another state.

◆ **Where the Jobs Are**

Specialized courses in credit are offered by banking and credit associations, public and private vocation schools and community colleges. Courses in finance and accounting can also prove helpful in getting hired and learning the job.

◆ **Training**

More women than men work as retail credit authorizers. But banks and financial services employ fairly equal numbers of men and women as credit checkers.

◆ **The Male/Female Equation**

◆ **Making Your Decision: What to Consider**

The Bad News

❏ Repetitious work
❏ Having to be on the phone all day
❏ Being confined to a desk and chair
❏ Relatively low salary (for some)

The Good News

❏ Wide geographic job availability
❏ Flexible scheduling sometimes available
❏ Part-time job opportunities
❏ Minimal skills required for entry

WHAT IT'S REALLY LIKE

Donna Otto, 33,
senior credit authorizer,
Chase Manhattan Bank, USA,
Wilmington, Delaware
Years in the field: seven

How did you become a credit authorizer?
I was going through a divorce and needed a job to support
myself. A neighbor who worked at Chase suggested I
apply for a job there. I was intimidated because I had been
out of the job market and my office experience was not
recent. But I got a clerical position in the bank card division.

What did you do on the job?
I assigned account numbers to new credit card accounts. I
had to look at each application to determine what type of
card the person was applying for and match it to the proper
account number. Then I would enter it into the computer. I
also did proofreading.

How did you learn to do the job?
All the teaching was done by supervisors and peers. We
had manuals, but I only used them as a reference on occa-
sion. In two weeks I could perform all the tasks without
help.

What was your next job?

After a year and a half on the job, I moved to credit investigations. I was responsible for calling the applicant if information was missing. I also verified information, for example by calling the employer listed to check the date the person started at the company and his or her income and job status. I also obtained a credit bureau report. I did this for two years. For several years after that, I did credit authorization work on lines of credit for businesses.

What is your current job?

Four months ago I was promoted to senior credit authorizer. I still do all the same work, but now I assist the supervisors by helping other staff members and training the new staff. I do an average of 120 to 130 applications a day.

What do you look for when making credit authorization decisions?

There are specific guidelines, which include late payment or balances not paid. The types of credit an applicant has as well as how long he or she has had them are also factors.

Is it difficult to make the decisions?

No, but there are some pitfalls. I have to make sure that the credit bureau history actually matches the applicant. If the social security number is off by one digit, the wrong credit report may have been pulled. Or it might be a case where a father and a son have the same name.

What do you like most about your job?

It is interesting because I learn a lot about people's spending habits. Also, I have discovered cases of fraud, which I turn over to our fraud department. Sometimes applicants create employment information or provide false social security numbers.

What type of person would perform well in this job?

It helps to know how to use a keyboard. I'm on the computer 90 percent of the day, and about 50 percent of the time I'm also on the phone. I have to be able to concentrate on what I am entering while talking to the person. I have to be pleasant and relaxed on the phone while asking for personal information. The job isn't stressful, but you have to use good judgment and basic common sense. And you must be accurate and thorough.

55

Penny Sylvester, 27,
senior mortgage loan processor,
First Fidelity Bancorporation,
North Brunswick, New Jersey
Years in field: four

How did you get into the mortgage business?
My first job was working as a receptionist for a mortgage company in Florida. I typed training manuals on how to become a mortgage broker. Within six months I moved up to a processor trainee. In about four months I could handle the basic mortgage cases, but it takes a year to really know how to process all the different types.

How were you trained?
Everything was done on-the-job, but typing all those training manuals helped! I also attended a few seminars on the mortgage business. You need the hands-on experience to really learn the process and the unique situations. For instance, a self-employed client requires different paperwork than one employed by a company. There were times I felt like quitting because there was so much to learn—I didn't think I would ever get it all. But I'm not a quitter.

What was your next job?
The company transferred me to Atlanta, Georgia, where I worked as a mortgage loan processor for a year and a half. By the time I left, I was a senior mortgage loan processor.

What is your current job?
I moved to New Jersey in September 1993 and interviewed with the mortgage division at First Fidelity Bancorporation. Because of my experience, I started as senior mortgage loan processor in the VIP mortgage division, which deals with very important people such as politicians, wealthy individuals and other important bank customers.

Describe your job.
My main responsibility is to make sure all the necessary paperwork on clients who have applied for a mortgage is in order so that the underwriters can decide whether to approve it. By the time I see a file, a mortgage sales representative has already met with or talked over the phone

with the clients to help them fill out the application and obtain the necessary documents.

I then obtain a credit history report on the clients and order an appraisal on the property. If everything checks out, I enter the information in the computer and prepare a disclosure statement, which the clients receive within three days of their meeting with the mortgage sales representative. It lists the terms of the mortgage and the other fees that the clients will be expected to pay at the closing.

I also check the property appraisal when it comes in to make sure the property value is comparable to other real estate in the neighborhood. When all the documents are in, I package the loan—put together all the necessary documentation—for the underwriter.

Do you ever talk with the client?
Once the sales representative hands the documents to me, I usually take over the client communication, most of which happens over the phone. I may have to ask them for missing information, and they are always calling me asking what the status of the situation is.

What is the hardest part of the job?
It is very stressful! There are 20 things going on at once, and I have to remember every detail for each client. And these are the VIP clients, so I have to be extra polite and thorough with my work. Depending on the volume, I can have a huge caseload of loans to process.

What type of person would do well in this job?
You have to be very personable, both on the phone and in person. You can never get upset or angry. You have to be flexible and pay attention to details. The learning curve is steep, but if you hang in there it is a great job.

What do you like about the job?
Well, it certainly isn't monotonous! I still feel as if I am learning something new every day. My clients become very special people to me, and I work evenings and weekends to get things done for them. After all, I know every detail of their financial, and sometimes personal, life. Sometimes after the mortgage closings, they send me flowers to thank me. That's really rewarding.

I can also make a lot of overtime pay. The best part is that I am an expert in a very competitive field. If I have to, I can work in any state for any bank or mortgage company. It is a very secure feeling to know I have marketable skills.

Tiffany Tallman, 25,
credit authorizer, Nordstrom, Denver, Colorado
Years in the field: six months

How did you become a credit authorizer?
I was working as a salesperson for Nordstrom in Los Angeles. My husband and I decided to move back to Denver, where we are originally from. After we relocated, I got a call from Nordstrom asking if I wanted to work in the credit authorization center here in Denver. I liked working for this company, so I accepted the offer.

How were you trained for the job?
My background in sales really helped me understand the job because I frequently had to call the authorization center to ask questions regarding customer accounts. I was trained by more experienced co-workers in credit authorization on how to answer those questions and more.

What are your job responsibilities?
Opening new accounts is the biggest one. A salesperson will call and give me basic information on the customer so that I can make a decision on whether to grant an instant account or not. I have the authority to make a decision, usually in about two minutes. It takes a lot of concentration to digest all the information and make an accurate judgment. If I'm not sure, I can get a second opinion from a supervisor. After awhile it gets easy, and you learn what to focus on and look for.

What else do you do?
On average, I handle about 160 calls a day, and the average call takes two minutes. There are two common types: questions about credit finance charges and requests for account closings. I get lots of calls from customers who claim they

paid their bill on time, but in the next month's billing they are charged a finance fee. I can check the date their bill arrived, and if it was within the due date, I can credit the finance charge to their account.

When customers call to request that their account be closed, I try to find out why and fix any problem. Sometimes I can, and they decide not to close their account.

Are your phone calls monitored?

Sometimes. We know that at any time a supervisor or manager could be monitoring our calls to make sure we are handling them properly. If we make "perfect" calls in terms of time constraints and responses to customers' requests, we can get a cash bonus.

What do you like best about your job?

Every call is different. Some can take up to 45 minutes to handle. I may have to do some research on a call and go look up receipts or other files on the account or confer with a supervisor. I also like voice-to-voice communications— it's both very private and somewhat intimate.

I work in a nice building that's quiet and comfortable. When a call comes in, my headset beeps. There's a cafeteria for the employees and even a gym I can join. I also like the fact that I don't take this job home with me.

What don't you like about your job?

Sometimes customers are angry and upset about something and usually take it out on me. I try to be calm and polite and help them resolve the problem. However, sometimes nothing will appease them. When I reach that point, I transfer the call to a supervisor. I also don't like sitting all day long, but at least I can get up and stretch or walk during my breaks.

Would you recommend this job to someone?

Yes, especially if you want flexibility in terms of when you work. Right now I am working Monday through Thursday and on Sunday. There are weekend hours, but it balances with other days off.

The trading floor of an exchange—sometimes called "the pit"— is a bustling, exciting place to work. Buy and sell orders must be placed in seconds or the asking price is lost. Runners and clerks make sure that clients' buy and sell orders are executed. If you like being at the center of intense action, you'll probably love being on the floor of an exchange.

Trade floor runners, who are sometimes called squad clerks or floor clerks, are employed either directly by a stock or commodities exchange or by securities firms, banks or brokerage houses that trade on an exchange.

The pit is mapped out in a very precise manner. It is made up of zones, wire rooms, trading desks and phone areas. Most exchanges have the floor personnel wear a uniform jacket of a specific color that designates their job.

Runners have to learn where everything is located so they can get to a designated location the fastest way possible. They wait in their assigned zone for instructions from a broker or trader or from the wire room. They then deliver the buy or sell order to a specialist in the firm's booth on the trading floor. After the trade is done, the broker gives the runner the filled order, or verification of the trade, and he delivers it back to the phone clerk. The pressure to get the transaction done at a certain price (by using your wits and your feet) is intense.

Since runners are at the bottom of the career ladder, don't be surprised if you are also asked to pick up lunch for the boss or get a round of coffee for the brokers.

But if your personality is suited to the pace and rough-and-tumble atmosphere and you prove yourself to be fast, competent and motivated, you'll no doubt find yourself being promoted to another floor position—sometimes in a matter of months.

Becoming a phone or data clerk is a common next step. In that job, most of your time will be spent on the phone talking with account executives (brokers) or their clients. It is your job to make sure that buy and sell orders from clients are relayed quickly to the specialists on the floor (usually by using a runner or hand signals). Even as a clerk, you'll spend most of the day on your feet.

Jobs are limited to certain geographic areas where exchanges are located, including New York, Chicago, Los Angeles, Boston, San Francisco and Philadelphia.

To be successful, you'll have to master procedures carefully, whether it's knowing where to go with a ticket or making sure that a transaction was successfully completed and recorded. But if the prospect of being a critical link in the chain of the exchange of securities or commodities excites you, the pit is probably the place for you.

What You Need to Know

❏ High school economics helpful but not necessary

Necessary Skills

❏ Math skills, especially calculating fractions
❏ Familiarity with computers

Do You Have What It Takes?

❏ Assertive personality and body language (you may have to push your way past people on the floor)
❏ Quick feet (to get to your designated area on time)
❏ Ability to follow directions swiftly and accurately
❏ Ability to stay calm under pressure
❏ Genuine interest in the business of Wall Street

Physical Requirements

❏ Well-groomed appearance
❏ Stamina to stay on your feet all day

◆ **Getting into the Field**

Job opportunities: highly competitive

Job openings are extremely limited because technology is replacing the need for people to physically deliver information. Jobs are also limited to cities that have a stock or commodities exchange. This is also one job where knowing someone "on the inside" is a definite plus in getting hired.

◆ **Job Outlook**

Entry-level jobs: runner, squad clerk

◆ **The Ground Floor**

On-the-Job Responsibilities

Beginners

❏ Receive buy and sell orders from phone clerk and deliver to brokerage firm representative or specialist on floor
❏ Return completed transaction slip from broker to phone clerk
❏ Answer phones and deliver messages to brokers
❏ Deliver reports to designated brokerage firm representative

Phone, Floor and Data Clerks

May do a combination of the following:
❏ Answer the phone and take messages
❏ Do light paperwork
❏ Tabulate closing figures at day's end
❏ Relay buy and sell orders from customers to brokers or specialists on the floor (often by using a runner or hand signals)
❏ Monitor prior day's trading activity for accuracy and make corrections
❏ Plot trading activity on chart
❏ Compile data for decision-making committee members who assign new stocks to specialists
❏ Monitor automated systems desk for problems coming through, such as a cancel order that was not executed, and send problem to appropriate area for correction

When You'll Work

Most exchanges are open from 9:30 A.M. to 4:00 P.M., Monday through Friday. Runners start their job the moment the floor opens and work through the day until it closes. They get time off for lunch, and if there is a slow period they can take breaks but cannot leave the floor. Brokerage firms may have runners work in shifts on the floor. Overtime is common, especially when the market is very active.

One or two weeks off after a year of full-time employment is common. And whenever the exchange is closed (major religious and federal holidays), you'll get the day off.

◆ **Time Off**

❏ Health care benefits for full-time employees

◆ **Perks**

◆ **Who's Hiring**

❏ Stock exchanges
❏ Commodities exchanges
❏ Brokerage houses and securities firms
❏ Banks that are member firms of an exchange

❏ Stress-related health problems
❏ Burnout from fast-paced activity
❏ Aching feet and lower back pain from standing all day

◆ **On-the-Job-Hazards**

Beginners and experienced runners: No potential for travel

◆ **Places You'll Go**

The pits of most exchanges are busy, crowded and noisy. There may be windows high above the floor, but most wall space is filled with computer screens that flash the current prices of stocks and bonds in bright green all day. The floor is filled with booths, wire rooms, brokerage firm booths, supervisor areas and lots of phones on posts in the middle of aisles. There are usually two floors to a trading floor. People shout constantly from one floor to another and across the floor.

◆ **Surroundings**

Starting salaries: $16,000-$20,000
Phone and data clerks: $25,000+
Salaries are lower in the Midwest and higher on the East and West Coasts. Most exchanges have a performance review every three to six months. By the end of nine months, a top performer can be earning $2,000 a month. Exchanges also offer temporary jobs, which in most cases are the same as full-time jobs but without the added health

◆ **Dollars and Cents**

coverage. Temporary runner positions can start at $12,000 and go up to $14,500 in six months. Temps can also receive a cash bonus of up to $600 every six months if their job performance is good.

Moving Up ◆   If you prove yourself dependable, a quick study and willing to pitch in to do whatever is needed, chances are you'll be tapped for another floor position. You may become a phone clerk and take calls from the brokers' clients and relay them to the specialists on the floor. Phone clerks start their positions with small money orders, then work their way up to taking orders worth hundreds of thousands of dollars. Advancement in this position is based on the amount of money you are responsible for.

Another option is becoming a price reporter; you'll track the trading activity and report it to the rest of the exchange. You can also be hired by a brokerage firm on the floor and work as a back office clerk, among other positions.

Some trade floor runners who have moved up the ranks decide to become registered representatives. You must first be sponsored by a brokerage firm and then pass an exam administered by the National Association of Securities Dealers, Inc. After you pass the exam, you get a Series 7 license. Many states also require that you pass the Uniform Securities Agents State Law Examination.

There are nine major exchanges in the United States:
- ❏ American Stock Exchange, New York, New York
- ❏ Boston Stock Exchange, Boston, Massachusetts
- ❏ Chicago Mercantile Exchange, Chicago, Illinois
- ❏ Chicago Board of Trade, Chicago, Illinois
- ❏ Chicago Stock Exchange, Chicago, Illinois
- ❏ Chicago Board of Options Exchange, Chicago, Illinois
- ❏ New York Stock Exchange, New York, New York
- ❏ Pacific Stock Exchange, San Francisco and Los Angeles, California
- ❏ Philadelphia Stock Exchange, Philadelphia, Pennsylvania

Securities and commodity firms and banks that are members of the exchange will be found in the same cities.

The majority are men.

The Bad News

- ❏ You'll be on your feet all day
- ❏ Still a male-dominated world
- ❏ Pressure to react quickly
- ❏ Low pay to start
- ❏ Job openings very limited

The Good News

- ❏ You're not confined to a desk
- ❏ On-the-job training provided
- ❏ Advancement opportunities
- ❏ Your adrenaline will pump
- ❏ There's rarely a dull moment

◆ **Where the Jobs Are**

◆ **The Male/Female Equation**

◆ **Making Your Decision: What to Consider**

WHAT IT'S REALLY LIKE

Albert Hering, 28,
phone clerk, member bank,
Chicago Mercantile Exchange,
Chicago, Illinois
Years in the field: seven

How did you get started in the field?
I worked at a paint factory during the summer to earn
money for college, but I had to quit after two years because
I wasn't earning enough. My brother-in-law was working
at the Chicago Mercantile Exchange and got me a job with
a member bank as a runner. Being on the floor of the
Exchange was so exciting—I loved it right away.

Did you receive any training for the job?
Most of the training is done on the job. I found that my
economics courses were helpful in understanding how the
markets worked, though.

What does a runner do?
Ironically, what we don't do is run—it's not allowed on the
trading floor because it's congested. My job was to take
order slips from the phone clerk and very quickly deliver
them to the broker in the trading pit who will make the
actual trade. The environment on the floor is chaotic;
everyone is yelling, pushing, shoving.

After the trade is done, the broker gives the runner the filled order, or verification of the trade, and he delivers it back to the phone clerk. The runner can also get instructions from a wire room operator to be delivered to a broker. Runners are also expected to get coffee for the boss and deliver lunch to the brokers when asked.

How do you prove yourself on this job?

One way is to learn to plot charts to help the brokers. I took a technical analysis course to learn this, but other firms teach their runners how to do it as part of their training. At the end of the day, I create a chart that shows the opening price of a stock and its high, low and closing price. By studying the chart, brokers can make predictions for the next day's market trends and pass them on to their customers.

How long were you a runner?

I was a runner for six months and then became a phone clerk. Some people remain runners for years, but others like me get lucky and move on quickly.

What do you do as a phone clerk?

I still work on the trading floor, but I am on the phone all day talking with my bank's account executives (brokers) or their customers to relay their buy and sell order to the specialists on the floor. I relay the order by using a runner or by using hand signals to get the information to the specialist. I stand in a two-foot-square space like a phone booth all day. It's not glamorous, but it is so exciting.

When do you work?

I work the 7 A.M. to 2 P.M. shift. But if the market has been really hectic or I need to speak to customers again, I work overtime in the bank office, where there is computer equipment that monitors market movement. I relay that information to customers who want to trade on the overseas markets.

What is the hardest part of your job?

The pressure. I must be able to think fast on my feet and make important decisions. The trade is made in seconds. If I miss that window of opportunity by hesitating for mere seconds, I've blown it for the customer.

What do you like most about the job?

The opportunities are endless. There are people right out of high school who have proven their abilities and worked their way up fast and are making lots of money. There are many levels to a phone clerk position. I started out with customers investing a few thousand and have moved up to dealing with customers who are investing millions. Even though I am still a phone clerk, my responsibilities are now greater because my customers are worth more. If I get my Series 3 license (which allows registered representatives to buy and sell commodities) and develop my own customers, the commissions I can make are unlimited.

What advice would you give people considering this field?

They must be able to work under pressure and deal with a high level of stress. They have to be persistent and some-what assertive to get the job done. If you don't have these skills or qualities, you won't be able to make it on the trading floor.

Belinda DaSilva, 27,
assistant supervisor of equity floor operations, Pacific Stock Exchange, San Francisco, California
Years in the field: seven

How did you get into the exchange?

I had been out of high school about 18 months and had a new baby to take care of. I needed a good job that offered a decent salary and good benefits. A friend told me about an opening for an equity floor clerk at the exchange, so I applied for the job and got it.

Did you have any background that helped prepare you?

No, but I got on-the-job training. I didn't have much experience with computers; I was familiar with the logging on and off, and the new software programs were fairly easy to learn. I did take a word processing course on my own, and it really helped.

What did you do as an equity floor clerk?

I worked from 4:30 A.M. to 1:00 P.M. The first hour of the day was spent getting the exchange's computerized trading system, called SCOREX, ready for trading. I turned on all the printers and made sure the shout down lines (our telephone system linkup to the Los Angeles exchange) were on. I also sent test messages to the Intermarket Trading System line that links all exchanges across the country to make sure it was on.

I spent the next hour helping the traders, who are called specialists and brokers, with any prior day's problems. We made sure trade tickets were available and put the buy blotter (a report of all the trades that took place on the previous day) together.

When the trading day began, at 6:30 A.M., my job was to pick up tickets from specialists and brokers, time stamp them, and deliver them to a data entry operator.

What was your next position?

After about two weeks, I was moved to the teletype department, the computerized transmission center where we sorted and filed trading tickets. We also took the comps off the printers and delivered them to the specialists and brokers. Comps are printed comparison tickets of how trades were entered on the exchange tape, allowing the person who did the trade to make any necessary corrections to the tape. We also sent reports to the Los Angeles Equity Floor and bonds to the clearing system.

What is your current position?

After about three years I was promoted to assistant supervisor of equity floor operations. I still come in at 4:30 A.M. to help open the floor for trading. I supervise and train the equity floor clerks and data entry operators.

What do you like about your job?

Well, my hours are great. I have three small children, and my husband works nights, so we don't need a baby-sitter. I am always meeting new people. Another great thing about the exchange is the opportunity for career advancement; available jobs within the exchange are posted regularly. But most important, the people here are great to work with.

What advice would you give someone thinking about working at the exchange?
Wear comfortable shoes! I am on my feet the majority of the time and don't have much of an opportunity to sit down. Also, you need to stay focused. The time element at the exchange can be critical, and there is no time for goofing around. You need to be able to perform a variety of tasks, and you need to be reliable and dependable.

Edward Slavin, 28,
data clerk, main trading desk,
American Stock Exchange,
New York, New York
Years in the field: two

How did you get started as a runner?
I had completed four years of service in the Air Force and needed a civilian job. A friend of mine who worked at the American Stock Exchange told me I fit all the basic requirements—personableness, reliability and an ability to follow instructions. So I interviewed and got the job.

What did you do on your first job?
The exchange uses different titles to describe the runner position. For example, I was assigned to a squad and was a sub-station data clerk. As a sub-station clerk, I was part of a five-member squad that supported 50 to 60 brokers. Every day I would be assigned to a trading post or other section of the floor. Sometimes I would be needed to fill in for other, similar positions. Runners have to be very flexible.

I had to learn where every assigned post and member firm was located and the shortest route to get there. Everything is open space. Everyone is always moving or shouting or waving paper around. Everyone at the exchange wears a jacket that is color coded so everyone knows what you do. Runners wear red, clerks wear black and supervisors wear brown.

My responsibility was to take the buy and sell order, in the form of a ticket, from the brokers and run it to the member firm's booth on the floor. These are brokerage firms that are members of the American Stock Exchange. I had to get the ticket to the booth in the most timely manner possible. Seconds can make or break a deal at the exchange, so I have to move fast. I am constantly on the move. When they want us they yell, "Squad!," and one of us goes over to receive the buy and sell ticket and instructions. We supported the brokers, but I reported to a supervisor who managed the squad. I was a squad runner for about a month and then became a data clerk at the main trading desk.

How were you trained?
On the job. I learned from either supervisors or other people doing the same functions. I always try to learn about the jobs being done around me so that if someone doesn't show up or they need extra help, I can step in.

What did your next job involve?
This desk acts as a central command post for the exchange. I did everything from answering the phone and taking messages to light paperwork such as tabulating closing day figures. I did everything my two supervisors asked me to do, and if one didn't have time to complete her tasks, I would help her get them done. Sometimes I helped with the payroll. I also began to monitor something called the "hoot and holler" line. When there was a halt on a specific stock, I picked up the phone and made a general announcement to the brokers that there has been a halt on trading of that stock.

What are you currently doing?
I am still a data clerk at the main desk, but my responsibilities have grown. I had some computer knowledge from my Air Force days, and when my supervisors realized I wanted to learn more, they encouraged me to experiment with their personnel system. With their help and my background in computers, I started to create personnel files on the computer, something they didn't have before on the trading desk. Keeping the files updated is now part of my job. One of the two supervisors left, and I started filling in and helping to perform supervisory functions unofficially. I still answer the phones, do the hoot and holler line, handle the

73

personnel files and tabulate the hours of the floor employees for payroll.

What advice would you give someone thinking about a job at the exchange?
You have to be a go-getter and look for the openings. Supervisors look for someone who can do the job accurately, fast and with no interference. For instance, a runner can't stop along the way to an assignment and chat with s omeone. That's noticed, and it isn't appreciated. You must be tough-skinned and flexible. People will yell at you, but you have to learn not to take it personally. It's a great job with plenty of advancement opportunities.

WILL YOU FIT INTO THE FINANCIAL WORLD?

Before you sign up for a program of study or start to look for one of the jobs described in this book, it's smart to figure out whether that career will be a good fit given your background, skills and personality. There are several ways to do this assessment, including:

❑ Talk to people who already work in that field. Find out what they like and don't like about their jobs, what kinds of people their employers hire, and what their recommendations are about training. Ask them if there are any books or publications that would be helpful for you to read. Maybe you could even "shadow" the workers for a day as they go about their duties.

❑ Use a computer to help you identify career options. Some of the most widely used software programs are *Discover,* by the American College Testing Service; *SIGI Plus,* developed by the Educational Testing Service; and *Careers,* by Peterson's. Some public libraries make this career software available to library users at little or no cost. The career counseling or guidance office of your high school or local community college is another possibility.

❏ Take a vocational interest test. The most common are the Strong Interest Inventory and the Kuder Occupational Interest Survey. High schools and colleges usually offer free testing to students and alumni at their guidance and career planning offices. Many career counselors in private practice or at community job centers can also give the test and interpret the results.

❏ Talk to a career counselor. You can find one by asking friends and colleagues if they know of any good ones. Or contact the career information office of the adult education division of a local college. Its staff and workshop leaders often do one-on-one counseling. The job information services division of major libraries sometimes offers low- or no-cost counseling by appointment. Or check the Yellow Pages under the heading "Vocational Guidance."

But first, before you spend time, energy or money doing any of the above, take one or more of the following five quizzes (one for each career discussed in the book). The results can help you begin to evaluate whether you have the basic traits and abilities that are important to success in that career—in short, whether you are cut out for it.

If a position as a bank teller interests you, take this quiz:

Read each statement below, then choose the number 0, 5 or 10. The rating scale below explains what each number means:

> **0** = Disagree
> **5** = Agree somewhat
> **10** = Strongly agree

___I am good at counting money and getting my own checkbook to balance

___I don't think I would get rattled if I was under pressure to serve many customers quickly

___I would feel comfortable being responsible for large amounts of cash

___I can handle several different kinds of tasks at the same time without losing track of details

___I get along well with many different types of people and am good at putting them at ease

___I think I could keep my cool even if customers were rude or difficult

___I like the idea of helping people solve their banking problems

___I am patient and wouldn't mind explaining the same information over and over to different customers

___I wouldn't mind being on my feet all day

___I am a fast learner and can quickly grasp new procedures

Now add up your score.   ___Total points

If your total points are less than 50, you may want to reconsider your priorities or re-evaluate your suitability for a career as a bank teller. If your total points are between 50 and 75, you may have what it takes to be a good bank teller, but be sure to do more investigation. If your total points are 75 or more, it's likely you have the interest and motivation to be a successful bank teller.

If a career as a securities sales assistant interests you, take this quiz:

Read each statement below, then choose the number 0, 5 or 10. The rating scale below explains what each number means.

0 = Disagree
5 = Agree somewhat
10 = Strongly agree

___I'm familiar with computers and feel I could learn how to use specialized programs easily

___The idea of working in a bustling, noisy work space appeals to me

___I am fascinated by or interested in learning more about the business of Wall Street

____It wouldn't bother me to work for more than one boss

____I've got a pleasant telephone manner and don't mind spending a lot of time on the phone

____I'm an organized type who keeps everything in its place

____The idea of researching problems and coming up with answers interests me

____I'm good at following instructions precisely

____I know how to file and retrieve information quickly

____I have good keyboarding skills

Now add up your score.   ____Total points

If your total points are less than 50, you probably don't have sufficient interest in the work of a sales assistant or the inclination to learn what's required. If your total points are between 50 and 75, you may have what it takes to be a good sales assistant, but be sure to do more investigation by following the suggestions at the beginning of this section. If your total points are 75 or more, it's likely you have the interest and motivation to be a successful sales assistant.

If a career as a tax preparer interests you, take this quiz:

Read each statement below, then choose the number 0, 5 or 10. The rating scale below explains what each number means.

0 = Disagree
5 = Agree somewhat
10 = Strongly agree

____I like the idea of seasonal work

____I do my own taxes or would like to learn how

____I have a good aptitude for working with numbers

____I'm good at putting people I don't know at ease and would feel comfortable talking to any type of client

____I know how to ask questions simply and directly

____I am a detail-oriented person

___I can enter information into a computer or feel I could learn to do so quickly

___I wouldn't mind doing repetitive work

___I'm good at explaining hard-to-understand information to others

___I am a good listener and can accurately take down information I hear

Now add up your score.   ___Total points

If your total points are less than 50, you may want to think twice about how good a match tax work is with your personality and skills. If your total points are between 50 and 75, you may have what it takes to be a good tax preparer, but you may need additional training. If your total points are 75 or more, it's likely you have the interest and motivation to be a successful tax preparer.

If a career as a credit checker interests you, take this quiz:

Read each statement below, then choose the number 0, 5 or 10. The rating scale below explains what each number means:

0 = Disagree
5 = Agree somewhat
10 = Strongly agree

___I wouldn't mind having most of my communication with customers over the phone

___Sitting for eight hours a day (with breaks) wouldn't bother me

___I am a good listener and can explain procedures and policies to customers

___I think I would be good at identifying missing information and following up to make sure it's completed

___I am good at assembling printed information into a file or form that can be easily understood by someone else

___I am persistent and could track down information that may be difficult to obtain

____I think I would be good at cross-checking information to make sure it is consistent

____I am good at working independently and setting my own work pace

____I get along with almost everyone and have a knack for calming down people who are upset

____I am familiar with computers or am willing to learn

Now add up your score.   ____Total points

If your total points are less than 50, you may not be suited for work as a credit checker. If your total points are between 50 and 75, you may have what it takes to be a good credit checker, but be sure to confirm your interest by following the suggestions at the beginning of this section. If your total points are 75 or more, it's likely you have the interest and motivation to be a successful credit checker.

If a career working on a trade floor interests you, take this quiz:

Read each statement below, then choose the number 0, 5 or 10. The rating scale below explains what each number means:

> **0** = Disagree
> **5** = Agree somewhat
> **10** = Strongly agree

____I like the idea of working in a noisy, busy "marketplace"

____The idea of being on my feet all day doesn't bother me

____I can follow instructions quickly and accurately

____I'm fascinated by the stock market

____I can be assertive, both physically and psychologically, to get my job done

____I wouldn't mind working for more than one boss

____I like the idea of being an important link in financial transactions

___I'm personable and get along with many types of
people

___I can be versatile and help out those around me, even if
it's not my job

___I can handle a very stressful work environment where
there is pressure every day to get things done

Now add up your score.   ___Total points

If your total points are less than 50, you may want to
re-evaluate your suitability for work as a trade floor runner
or clerk. If your total points are between 50 and 75, you
may have what it takes, but be sure to do more investigat-
ing. If your total points are 75 or more, it's likely you have
the interest and motivation to be a successful trade floor
runner.

ABOUT THE AUTHOR

Gail W. Kislevitz is a former speech writer and director of communications in the banking industry. Her 15 years in banking also included positions in recruitment and public relations. She was a contributing writer and researcher for the book *Career Choices for M.B.A.s*. A member of the YWCA's Academy of Women Achievers, Gail is currently a freelance writer residing in Ridgewood, New Jersey.

This book is dedicated to Beatrice Maleady Waesche, my role model, who was the most successful and loving mother a daughter could have.

A big thanks to Androc, Elijah and Anna for allowing me to monopolize the computer and phone for the past few months. Your support and encouragement will be rewarded.